j973.049 Worthylake, Mary M.
WOR
   The Pomo.

$16.60

DATE			
SEP 1 0 1994		DEC 2 1 1996	
DEC 3 1994		FEB 1 3 1997	
OCT 3 1 1995		MAR 5 1997	
NOV 4 1995		MAY 6 1997	
NOV 3 0 1995		OCT 0 8 1997	
FEB 6 1996		NOV 0 6 1997	
JUN 1 8 1996		FEB 2 4 1999	
OCT 1 3 1996			
OCT 1 6 1996			

A New True Book

THE POMO

By Mary M. Worthylake

CHILDRENS PRESS®

CHICAGO

Rattles made from deer hooves
were used in some Pomo ceremonies.

PHOTO CREDITS

© Reinhard Brucker–11 (bottom left), 37;
Milwaukee Public Museum, 8 (right),
11 (right), 13 (left), 22, 27, 28 (2 photos);
Field Museum, Chicago, Cover Inset, 2, 7, 9,
11 (top left), 12 (bottom right), 13 (right), 15,
19, 20, 25 (3 photos), 26 (2 photos), 31, 33,
34, 35

Courtesy of the Grace Hudson Museum, City
of Ukiah, Ca. Collection of the Grace
Hudson Museum, Acc.# 8816. Pomo acorn
storage basket made by Joe Beatty.
Collected in 1908 near Ukiah, Ca. by
anthropologist John W. Hudson. The basket
is part of the Culin collection at the Brooklyn
Museum in New York–8 (left)

North Wind Picture Archives–16

PhotoEdit–© Alan Oddie, Cover; © Tony
Freeman, 39; © Deborah Davis, 44

Photri–© Arnold J. Kaplan, 40

SuperStock International, Inc.–© Ed
Cooper, 5

UPI/Bettmann–43

Valan–© Murray O'Neill, 12 (left); © Dennis
W. Schmidt, 12 (top right); © J. A. Wilkinson,
17 (left); © Val & Alan Wilkinson, 17 (right)

Tom Dunnington–Map, 4

COVER: Clear Lake area

COVER INSET: Pomo basket for acorn meal

Project Editor: Fran Dyra
Design: Margrit Fiddle

Library of Congress Cataloging-in-Publication Data

Worthylake, Mary M.
  The Pomo / by Mary M. Worthylake.
    p.   cm.–(A New true book)
  Includes index.
  ISBN 0-516-01057-3
  1. Pomo Indians–History–Juvenile literature.
2. Pomo Indians–Social life and customs–Juvenile
literature. [1. Pomo Indians. 2. Indians of North
America.] I. Title.
E99.P65W67   1994
973'.04975–dc20   93-36666
                                                  CIP
                                                  AC

TABLE OF CONTENTS

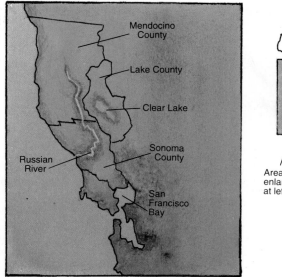

POMO HOMELANDS

The Pomo were one of the largest and best-known Native American tribes in California. Their land began at the Russian River north of San Francisco Bay. It included what today are Sonoma,

The Russian River flows through the hills of northern California.

Mendocino, and Lake counties. North of the Russian River, several hundred small Pomo villages stood on riverbanks and were clustered all around Clear Lake.

5

Although the strip of giant redwood trees along the Pacific coast was on their territory, the Pomo preferred to live in the sunny valleys to the east. They journeyed to the ocean only to gather seafood and clamshells.

The valleys and oak-covered hills provided them with food, and the rivers and streams teemed with fish.

This scene from a museum shows Pomo women gathering acorns.

SEED GATHERERS

Acorns were the main food of the Pomo. Women gathered the acorns in woven baskets. The baskets were carried on their backs and supported by a strap across their foreheads. The acorns

A huge basket on posts (left)
was used to store acorns.
Above: A small Pomo basket with
acorns from black oak trees

were stored in a huge
basket raised on posts.
    Much work was needed
to make the acorns edible.
8 First they were shelled.

These tools were used to pound acorns into a flourlike meal.

Then the kernels were
pounded into a flourlike
meal. Water was poured
over the meal to take
away the bitter taste. The
meal was then mixed with
water and cooked in
tightly woven baskets. Hot

9

rocks were dropped into the baskets to cook the meal into mush. The acorn mush was eaten with spoons made of elk horn. The acorn meal was also molded into a flat cake and baked on hot rocks.

The women used woven seed beaters to gather the seeds of grasses and wild grain. They used sharp digging sticks to reach edible roots and bulbs. In

Left: A Pomo seed beater
Below left: The bulbs
and roots of plants were
used for food.
Below: A Pomo basket filled
with manzanita berries

autumn, they went into
the hills to gather ripe
berries. The berries were
then dried and mixed with
the acorn mush.

11

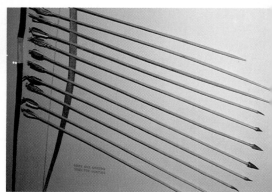

The Pomo used bows and
arrows (bottom right) to hunt
animals such as elk (above).
They used traps to
catch quail (top right).

The men hunted deer
and elk with bows and
arrows. All year round,
they hunted or trapped
small game such as
rabbits or quail. Fish traps

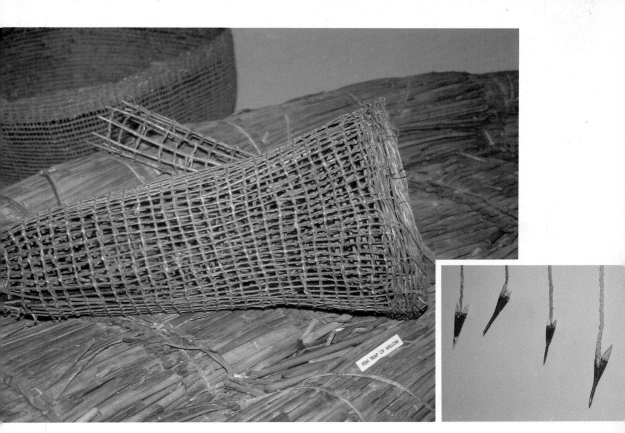

The Pomo caught fish in woven willow fish traps (left).
Sometimes they used fishhooks made of bone (right).

were set in Clear Lake
and in the rivers and
streams to catch fish.

With such an abundance
and variety of food, the
people seldom went hungry.

SHELTER

Pomo houses were used mainly by women and children for storing food, cooking, eating, and sleeping.

The Pomo built houses by sinking a circle of poles in the ground. The poles were bent together at the top and tied with strong vines. Bunches of long grass or reeds were

Pomo houses
were built
of poles and
grasses.

then tied to the frame.
When they were finished,
the houses looked like
upside-down baskets.

Usually only six or eight
families lived in a Pomo

A Pomo sweathouse

village, but there were a few larger settlements.

Each village had a sweathouse built over a pit. The outside was covered with sod. The men gathered every day for a sweat bath, and often slept in the sweathouse.

Many kinds of delicious berries, such as elderberries (left) and blackberries (right), grew in the hills and valleys of the Pomo homeland.

The women and children spent their time roaming through the hills and valleys gathering food. On these trips, they often camped under shelters of mats supported by poles.

17

CLOTHING

In their warm climate, the Pomo needed little clothing. The men wore a loincloth. The women wore a skirt. Skirts were sometimes made of deerskin, but more often they were made of fibers from rushes or shredded redwood or willow bark.

The Pomo usually went barefoot and bareheaded. The men sometimes wore earrings made of decorated bird bones or rods tipped with feathers or beads.

A Pomo cape made from rabbit fur

19

Museum scene showing a Pomo reed raft. The men at right are holding a woven fish trap.

BOATS

Unlike the Northern Coast tribes, the Pomo did not build boats that could ride the ocean waters. They tied bunches of reeds together to form rafts, which they used on Clear Lake. Simple log rafts helped them cross rivers.

MAKING MONEY

The Pomo were unusual among Native Americans in that they made "money" from the shells of sea animals.

First, the shells were broken into small pieces. Holes were bored in the middle, and the pieces were rounded and polished against a rough rock. Then they were threaded onto a string.

The shells were strung

Pomo shell "money" looked like strings of beads.

in groups of ten and given a certain value. They were used in trading with other tribes for deerskins, nuts, paints, and bows and arrows.

In the hills near Cache Creek, the Pomo mined a stone called magnesite. They made the magnesite into beads. When the stone beads were baked and polished, they shone with lovely colors of yellow, pink, and red. These beads were highly prized, and valued like precious gems.

BASKETS

Pomo baskets were among the finest made anywhere. The Pomo had no pottery, so their baskets served many purposes. There were big carrying baskets, tightly woven cooking baskets, and baskets for storing food. The men made some

The Pomo made special baskets
for different purposes. Flat
ones (above) were used for tossing
seeds to separate them from
their hulls. Round, deep baskets
(bottom right) stored fish, and baskets
with handles (bottom left) were
used for carrying things.

Pomo men made woven fish traps (left) and baby cradles (right).

of the simpler baskets that
were used as fish traps,
seed beaters, trays, and
baby cradles. The women
wove the finer baskets,

A beautifully made storage basket shows the artistry of the Pomo women.

such as the ornamented, watertight cooking baskets and patterned ones used for storage.

Pomo basket-makers were unusual in their use of twining and coiling. The

Pomo baskets were often decorated with feathers.

finest baskets, made for show or for gifts, were coiled. Some of these were decorated with feathers—black plumes from the quail or red feathers from the woodpecker.

The baskets were made of willow, pine, sedgeroot, and redbud. Thirty wrappings to an inch make a fine basket, but Pomo baskets sometimes had sixty or even more wrappings. The variety of patterns, the feathers and beads, and the fine workmanship show that Pomo women were excellent artists.

GAMES

The Pomo played a game
that the French settlers
came to call *lacrosse.* The
game is played with two
teams trying to hit the ball
across the opposing team's
goalpost. It is played with
a ball and a stick–or
crosse–made of bent wood
with a net at one end for
catching, carrying, or
throwing the ball.

The Pomo also played
a game with a bundle of

Pomo girls played
with toy dolls
and cradleboards
like these.

small sticks, one of which
had a special mark on it.
One player hid the sticks
behind his back and the
others guessed which hand
held the marked stick.

31

CEREMONIES

The larger villages had a meeting house, where people from different villages gathered for special ceremonies, dances, or "sings." When boys were about twelve years old, they spent several weeks in this house learning the history of the tribe, its dances, and its songs. At the end

Pomo whistles were used to make music for dancing.

of this time, the boys were initiated into the tribe in a special ceremony.

The Pomo had many ceremonial dances—some

This wand decorated with feathers was used in Pomo ceremonies.

sacred and some based on myths. One was the Dama ceremony, which took four days and featured acrobatic stunts. There was also a thunder dance and a coyote ceremony. In many such

A feather
headdress was
worn by the
dancers in Pomo
ceremonies.

rituals, the dancers were painted or wore costumes made of feathers and quills. They usually hid their faces with a bunch of twigs.

POMO BELIEFS

The Pomo believed in a wise Great Spirit called Madumda, who lived in the sky. His younger brother was called Coyote. There are many legends about Coyote, who was

The coyote looks like a small wolf. Many Native American nations have stories that tell about this clever and tricky animal.

fond of playing tricks and making mischief.

Some of these legends tell how he made a sun to light the world, brought fire, created humans, and changed animals into their present forms.

A Pomo legend tells of a hot season when the creeks dried up and the rains did not come. Swarms of grasshoppers ate the grass and the seeds, and the people were hungry. Coyote showed his love for the people by going to a damp place in the middle of a dried-up pond. He dug and dug until water began seeping up. He dug harder, and soon the water flowed fast, until it

The Pomo homeland had many beautiful rivers and streams.

filled up the pond and spread out to make Clear Lake. The grasshoppers came to the lake to drink, and Coyote turned them into fish. In this way, he brought food and water to the Pomo.

Californians act out Juan Cabrillo coming ashore during his exploration of the Pomo homeland in 1542.

THE POMO TODAY

When Europeans first came to California, it is estimated that the Pomo people numbered about 8,000. The census of 1910 showed that only 1,200 were left. Today, the population is increasing. The 1980 census listed 800 Native Americans in Lake County and almost 2,400 in Mendocino County. The Sonoma County census showed

3,500 American Indians, but these are probably not all Pomo.

Most Pomo live in small areas called *rancherias* rather than on large reservations. *Rancherias* are ruled by a group of elders, or councilmen. There are seven *rancherias* in Lake County alone.

A few of the older Pomo women still make baskets,

Molly Green was photographed in 1935 making the traditional Pomo baskets.

but the quality is not equal to that of their ancestors. The old baskets may be seen in historical museums at Ukiah or Lakeport.

The rolling green hills of the Clear Lake area
made up the heart of the Pomo lands.

Of course, strings of clamshells are no longer needed for trade money.

Today, Pomo live in modern houses and do the same kinds of work as other Americans. But the old stories, songs, and dances live on. The Pomo have not forgotten the traditions of their ancestors.

WORDS YOU SHOULD KNOW

abundance (ah • BUN • dince)–more than enough; a good supply

acorn (A • korn)–the nutlike seed of an oak tree

acrobatic (ak • ruh • BAT • ik)–doing tumbling and other tricks like an acrobat

ancestor (AN • sess • ter)–a grandparent or other forebear earlier in history

census (SEN • suss)–a counting of the number of people who live in a country

ceremony (SAIR • ih • moh • nee)–a celebration or a religious service

climate (KLYE • mit)–the average kind of weather at a certain place

coyote (kye • OH • tee)–a wild animal that looks like a small wolf

edible (ED • ih • bil)–good to eat

fibers (FYE • berz)–tough, stringy plant parts

initiate (in • ISH • ee • ait)–to make someone a member of a group

kernel (KER • nil)–the inside of a seed; the part that is good to eat

lacrosse (la • KRAWSS)–a game played by teams who try to get a ball into a goal using long sticks with a net at one end

magnesite (MAG • nih • site)–a white, yellowish, or brown mineral

mischief (MISS • chif)–pranks; playful tricks

precious (PRESH • uss)–having great value; rare

quill (KWILL)–the long, thin shaft of a feather

rancheria (ran • CHAIR • ee • ya)–a small settlement of Pomo Indians

redbud (RED • bud)–a small tree

reeds (REEDZ)–plants with strong, stiff stems that grow in water

reservation (reh • zer • VAY • shun)–land set aside for people to live on

rushes (RUSH • iz)–water plants with long, stiff stems

sedgeroot (SEJ • root)–a grasslike plant

shelter (SHEL • ter)–a place where people go to get away from the weather

sod (SAHD)–a block of soil that is bound together by grass roots

teem (TEEM)–to swarm; to be plentiful

traditions (truh • DISH • unz)–customs and beliefs; old ways of doing things

variety (vuh • RYE • ih • tee)–a number of different kinds

INDEX

About the Author

Mary M. Worthylake lives in California. She began researching the history of the Pomo years ago.